Adventures in Numeracy

Knights in Armour

Sally Hewitt

illustrated by Serena Feneziani

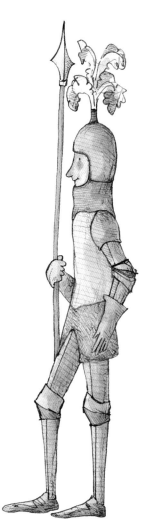

Belitha Press

Measure with the knights

The cock crows over the silent castle.
Everyone hurries to prepare for the big day.
But where are the knights and their pages?

The king is holding a tournament.
Help the pages to find armour, horses
and weapons for the knights.

Find out which knight shoots his arrow
the furthest, who is the heaviest, and
who needs the biggest horse.

The pages serve at the banquet. Help them fill
plates and baskets with food, and jugs with drink.

Afterwards, the pages are tired. Find them asleep
in the kitchen – under the table, behind the sacks
and between the barrels. Can you tell which
two knights are the last to go to bed?

The sun rises over the castle.

Everyone is asleep. What will
happen when the cock crows?

Everyone wakes up and starts to prepare for tournament day.

Find the king with his two servants.
Find three gatekeepers and four horsemen.

'What a beautiful day for a tournament!' says the king.

Can you find groups of five, six, seven, eight, nine and ten people?

The ten pages have a lot to do.

How many are asleep? How many are awake?
How many are wearing hats?

Time to get dressed!

Where are the missing hat, belt, tunic and leggings? Can you match the shoes?

Now it's time to dress the knights.

Match the knights to these words:

gigantic   tall   wide   old

tiny   short   thin   young

The knights wear armour for the tournament.

Help the pages find a shield and
a suit of armour to fit each knight.

Now they need weapons.

The tallest knight has the tallest spear.
Find the right spear for the shortest knight.

The twins are the same size.

Which two swords, two daggers and
two shields are the same size?

The knights line up to be inspected by the king.

Point to the knights in height order.
Start with the tallest.

'You're in the wrong order!'
he shouts.

Which knights are taller than the thinnest
knight? Which knights are shorter?

The ladies will watch the tournament.

Whose hats are too wide to go
through the narrow door?

Someone has sent them roses.

Who has five roses? Who has one more than five? Who has one less?

The tournament begins with an archery contest.

How many arrows have not gone far enough?

One of the knights
needs more practice!

How many arrows have gone too far?
Who is winning the contest?

The knights are weighed before the joust.

Who is the heaviest?
Who is the lightest?

There are four horses
for four of the knights.

Which horse should each knight choose?
Can you say why?

The knights charge in on the wrong horses.

Find the right horse for each knight.

They can't joust unless they change lances.

Find the lance that is the
right length for each knight.

All the knights take part in the horse race.

Who is winning? Who is in third place?
Who is coming last?

The crowds cheer on the riders.

Who is in front of the thinnest knight?
Who is behind him?

In the kitchens, the cooks prepare the banquet.

Which is the best basket for the apples?
Which is the best plate to put the turkey on?

The banquet is ready!

Have the pages chosen the best
plate and basket to carry the food?

After the tournament the knights
are hungry and thirsty.

Who doesn't have enough food?
Who has too much?

The pages bring them food and drink. What a feast!

How many glasses are empty?
How many are half full?

The pages have worked hard all day.

One page falls asleep on the table. Another is in front of the fire. Where are the others?

It's bedtime for the knights.

How many knights are going upstairs?
How many are already asleep?

One by one, the lights
go out in the castle.

Two knights are still awake.
Do you know who they are?

Notes for parents and teachers

tall

gigantic

Knights in Armour will help your child to:

- Learn and use words about measuring.
- Match and compare different sizes.
- Use concepts such as enough, not enough and too much.

- Learn and use words to describe position.
- Combine two groups of numbers and begin to add.
- Sort things into sets.

We meet the ten knights on tournament day. They are many sizes: gigantic, tiny, tall, short, wide, thin, and the same size (two pairs of twins). Help the pages to find armour, weapons and horses that are the right size for the knights.

young twins

Pages 8–27 are full of measuring activities:

tiny

- Match the knights to the word that best describes them.
- Put the knights in height order.
- Learn about heavy and light.

- Find which arrows have gone too far and which not far enough.
- Learn about capacity – how much food and drink will different-sized plates, baskets and jugs hold?

short

Pages 4–5 and 29 have different number activities. Count the cooks, guards and ladies preparing the castle for tournament day. After the feast, count the knights already asleep and those on their way to bed.

wide

Try these games and activities to help you learn about everyday measuring.

- Line up in height order: arrange your friends or family in order of height, with the tallest first. Then start with the shortest.

- Longest and shortest: cut strips of paper into different lengths. Point to the longest and shortest.

- Heavy and light: feel the weight of some fruit in your hand. Guess which are heavier and which are lighter. Weigh them to find out if you were right.

- Containers and capacity: play with plastic containers of different sizes and shapes in the bath. Pour water from one to the other to find out how much each holds.

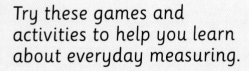

old twins

thin

First published in the UK in 2000 by

 Belitha Press Limited, London House,
Great Eastern Wharf, Parkgate Road,
London SW11 4NQ

Copyright © Belitha Press Limited 2000
Text copyright © Sally Hewitt 2000
Illustrations by Serena Feneziani

Series editor: Mary-Jane Wilkins
Editor: Russell McLean
Designers: Jamie Asher, Zoe Quayle
Educational consultant: Andrew King

ISBN 1 84138 217 5 (hardback)
ISBN 1 84138 221 3 (paperback)

Printed in China

British Library Cataloguing in
Publication Data for this book is
available from the British Library.

10 9 8 7 6 5 4 3 2 1